THE ART OF THE PIVOT

How to Navigate Change and Build Successful Products

CONFIDENCE EGBU

ISBN: 978-2-3878-3314-3

Publishing by:
Emphaloz Publishing House
Abuja, Nigeria.

www.emphaloz.com
publish@emphaloz.com

Published 2023

Cover Design by Emphaloz Digital

A catalogue record of this book will be available from the National Library of Nigeria.

PREFACE

In today's fast-paced and ever-evolving business landscape, the ability to adapt and pivot is more crucial than ever. The digital age has brought about rapid changes in technology, consumer behavior, and market dynamics, making it imperative for businesses to remain agile and responsive. "The Art of the Pivot: How to Navigate Change and Build Successful Products" is a timely and invaluable guide for product managers, entrepreneurs, and business leaders who seek to thrive in this dynamic environment. As someone who has spent decades in the industry, I have witnessed firsthand the transformative power of a well-executed pivot. Companies that have successfully navigated significant changes often emerge stronger, more resilient, and better positioned for long-term success. Conversely, those that resist change or fail to adapt often struggle to stay relevant and competitive. This book provides a comprehensive roadmap for understanding when and how to pivot, ensuring that your product and business remain on the cutting edge.

One of the key strengths of this book is its practical approach to the complexities of pivoting. It does not merely offer theoretical insights but delves deep into actionable strategies and frameworks that can be applied in real-world scenarios. From identifying the need for a pivot to gathering and analyzing data, from crafting a compelling new market position to managing stakeholders effectively, each chapter is packed with valuable information and tools that can help guide your pivot journey. The emphasis on data-driven decision-making is particularly noteworthy. In an age where data is abundant, leveraging it effectively to inform your pivot strategy can make the difference between success and failure. The chapters on metrics and measuring success provide a clear framework for tracking the impact of your pivot, allowing you to make informed adjustments and continually optimize your product.

Another highlight of this book is its focus on the human aspect of pivoting. Change can be challenging, not only for leaders but also for teams and stakeholders. The chapters on communication, stakeholder management, and fostering a culture of experimentation and continuous learning address these challenges head-on. They offer practical advice on how to lead through change, maintain team morale, and build a resilient, innovative organization. The inclusion of real-world case studies adds another layer of depth and relatability to the book. Learning from the successes and failures of companies like Slack, Netflix, and Amazon provides valuable insights and inspiration. These case studies demonstrate that pivoting is not just about changing direction but about strategic evolution and continuous improvement.

As you embark on the journey of navigating change and building successful products, I encourage you to approach it with an open mind and a willingness to embrace uncertainty. The insights and strategies presented in this book will equip you with the knowledge and confidence to pivot effectively, turning challenges into opportunities and laying the foundation for sustained success. In closing, "The Art of the Pivot" is a must-read for anyone looking to master the art of navigating change in today's volatile business environment. Its blend of practical advice, strategic frameworks, and real-world examples makes it an indispensable resource for product managers, entrepreneurs, and business leaders alike. May this book serve as your guide and companion as you chart a course toward innovation, growth, and success.

TABLE OF CONTENTS

INTRODUCTION

EMBRACING THE POWER OF CHANGE

Imagine pouring your heart and soul into creating a product. You've thoroughly researched the market, created an appealing design, and launched with a bang. But then a sinking feeling takes over. User engagement isn't what you expected, sales are flat, and the market appears to be shifting beneath you. Many businesses fear this moment: the realisation that their initial course of action may not be successful. In today's fast-paced business environment, sticking to a static strategy can be a recipe for disaster. The ability to adapt, adjust, and pivot is no longer a luxury; it is a necessity. Companies such as Instagram, which started as a photo-sharing app called Burbn, and Netflix, which was once a DVD rental service, demonstrate the power of a well-executed pivot.

This book, "The Art of the Pivot," is your roadmap to navigating change and emerging stronger on the other side. We'll delve into the why and how of successful pivots, equipping you with the knowledge and tools to identify the need for change, gather valuable insights, and lead your team through a smooth transition. Whether you're a seasoned product manager or a passionate entrepreneur with a fledgling idea, this guide will prepare you to embrace the inevitable twists and turns of the product development journey. The journey of building a product is rarely a straight path. Market conditions evolve, customer needs shift, and new technologies emerge. In such a dynamic environment, the ability to pivot—altering your strategy to meet new challenges and opportunities—is critical. The most successful companies are those that view change not as a threat but as an opportunity for innovation and growth.

Think about Instagram and Netflix. Instagram began as Burbn, a check-in app with a popular photo-sharing feature for users. Recognising this, the founders pivoted to focus solely on photo-sharing, giving birth to the Instagram we know today. Netflix transitioned from a DVD rental service to a streaming behemoth, anticipating the shift in media consumption habits. These pivots were more than just shifts in direction; they were strategic decisions that propelled these companies to new heights.

What This Book Offers

"The Art of the Pivot" will guide you through the entire process of executing a successful pivot. Here's what you can expect to learn:

- The psychological shift needed to view change as an opportunity, not a threat.
- Frameworks for recognizing the telltale signs that a pivot might be necessary.
- User research techniques and data analysis methods to inform your pivot strategy.
- Effective communication strategies to lead your team through change with clarity and purpose.
- Frameworks for prioritization and resource allocation during a pivot.
- The art of repositioning your product for a new target audience or market.
- Metrics and tracking tools to measure the success of your pivot.
- Strategies for fostering a culture of experimentation and continuous learning within your team.

- Inspiring real-world case studies of successful pivots across different industries.

The primary purpose of this book is to equip product managers, entrepreneurs, and business leaders with the knowledge and tools necessary to navigate change effectively. By the end of this book, you will have a comprehensive understanding of the strategies involved in making successful pivots, the importance of data-driven decision-making, and how to manage stakeholders and resources during times of change. Whether you are dealing with a sudden market shift, a technological disruption, or a strategic misstep, this book will guide you through the process of turning challenges into opportunities.

The ability to pivot effectively can be the difference between the success and failure of a product or even an entire business. By embracing change and viewing it as an opportunity rather than a threat, you can navigate the complexities of the modern business landscape with confidence. This book will serve as your guide through the art of the pivot, providing you with the insights and tools needed to turn challenges into opportunities and build successful products that stand the test of time. Are you ready to embrace the art of the pivot?

CHAPTER 1

THE PIVOT MINDSET:

Embracing Change as a Competitive Advantage

The business landscape is constantly shifting. New technologies emerge, consumer preferences shift, and entire industries can be disrupted seemingly overnight. In this dynamic environment, the ability to adapt and pivot is a key differentiator between success and failure. This chapter explores the pivot mindset—a way of thinking that sees change as an opportunity for growth. We'll look at the value of agility and adaptability, analyse the changing landscape of technology and markets, and see how pivoting can be a strategic tool for success. We'll also discuss the psychological aspects of accepting change and overcoming resistance within yourself and your team.

The Importance of Agility and Adaptability.

Imagine a ship sailing towards a specific destination. In calm seas, a rigid course might be sufficient. However, when storms roll in and currents shift, the ability to adjust course becomes paramount. The same principle applies to product development. In today's fast-paced business environment, clinging to a static strategy can be a recipe for disaster. Companies that remain agile and adaptable can seize new opportunities and navigate uncertainties more effectively.

Agility is important for many reasons. For starters, it reduces the time to market. Being adaptable allows businesses to respond quickly to market trends and seize new opportunities. This responsiveness can mean the difference between being a market leader and trailing the competition. Second, agility promotes innovation. A willingness to experiment and iterate fosters an innovative culture, which results in the development of cutting-edge products. Companies can improve and evolve continuously by remaining open to new ideas and approaches.

"The only sustainable competitive advantage is your organization's ability to learn and adapt faster than the competition." - Peter Drucker, Management Consultant

Agility also leads to higher customer satisfaction levels. Companies that stay agile can continuously adapt their products to meet changing customer needs and expectations. This adaptability ensures that products remain relevant and valuable to users, thereby increasing customer loyalty and satisfaction. Finally, agility promotes resilience. In a dynamic market, unexpected challenges are unavoidable. Agility enables businesses to weather storms and adapt to changing conditions, ensuring their long-term survival and success.

The Changing Landscape of Technology and Markets

The rate of technological advancement is accelerating, and consumer behaviour is changing rapidly. These changes necessitate a more flexible approach to product development. Companies must be prepared to pivot their strategies in order to stay current with trends and meet their customers' ever-changing demands.

Technological advancements have the potential to generate new opportunities while also disrupting established markets. For example, the proliferation of smartphones and mobile apps changed the way people interacted with technology, resulting in the emergence of entirely new industries. Companies that recognised these shifts and adjusted their strategies were able to seize new opportunities, whereas those that did not pivot were left behind.

Similarly, consumer behaviour is constantly changing. Today's customers expect personalised experiences, seamless interactions, and instant gratification. Companies must remain responsive to changing expectations and be prepared to pivot their strategies to meet them. This could include implementing new technologies, experimenting with different business models, or reimagining product offerings.

Pivoting as a Strategic Tool for Success

Pivoting is more than just a reactive response to challenges; it can also be a proactive strategy for capitalising on new opportunities and driving growth. Successful pivots require recognising when a change is required, gathering valuable insights, and carrying out the pivot with precision.

Take Instagram as an example. Instagram began as Burbn, a location-based check-in app, but later shifted its focus to photo sharing and social networking after realising that these features were particularly appealing to users. This strategic pivot resulted in phenomenal success, cementing Instagram's position as one of the world's most popular social media platforms.

Netflix provides another compelling example. What began as a DVD rental service by mail has grown into a streaming behemoth, revolutionising how we consume entertainment. Netflix's ability to anticipate changes in consumer preferences and adapt its business model enabled it to dominate the market and set the standard for streaming services.

Slack's story is also worth telling. Slack began as an internal tool for a game development company, but its flexibility allowed it to evolve into a popular workplace communication platform. This pivot was motivated by the realisation that the tool had broader applications and could meet a significant market need.

These examples showcase how embracing change and adopting a pivot mindset can lead to extraordinary outcomes. By viewing pivots as strategic tools rather than last-resort measures, companies can unlock new opportunities and achieve sustainable success.

The Psychological Aspects of Embracing Change

Change can be uncomfortable, and resistance to change is a natural human response. However, overcoming this resistance is crucial for cultivating a pivot mindset. Developing a pivot mindset involves embracing change, encouraging experimentation, and fostering a culture of continuous learning.

Adopting a growth mindset is essential for embracing change. A growth mindset sees challenges as opportunities to learn and grow. It encourages people to see failure as valuable learning experiences that lead to future success. By instilling a growth mindset in your team, you can foster an environment in which change is viewed positively and embraced as a means of improvement.

Developing a pivot mindset also requires encouraging experimentation. Create an environment in which team members feel comfortable experimenting and taking calculated risks. Reward creativity and innovative thinking, and put in place processes that enable rapid prototyping and feedback loops. This approach facilitates the rapid testing and refinement of ideas based on real-world insights.

Fostering continuous learning is essential for maintaining agility and adaptability. Invest in learning and development opportunities for your team, such as workshops, conferences, and training sessions. Encourage team members to acquire new skills and knowledge, and promote a culture of lifelong learning. Utilizing data analytics to gain insights into customer behavior, market trends, and product performance can also support continuous learning and inform data-driven decisions.

Implementing the Pivot Mindset in Your Organization

To successfully implement a pivot mindset within your organization, secure commitment from top leadership to champion agility and adaptability. Leaders should model the pivot mindset and encourage it at all levels of the organization. Foster collaboration across departments to ensure diverse perspectives and expertise are integrated into decision-making processes. This enhances the quality of insights and strategies.

Maintain open lines of communication with your team. Keep them informed about the reasons for pivots, the expected outcomes, and their roles in the process. Transparency builds trust and alignment, ensuring that everyone is on the same page. Design flexible processes that can accommodate changes without significant disruptions. Agile project management methodologies, such as Scrum or Kanban, can be particularly effective in managing pivots.

Adopting a pivot mindset is not just about being reactive to changes; it's about being proactive and viewing change as an integral part of the business strategy. By embracing agility and adaptability, companies can turn potential threats into opportunities, drive innovation, and achieve sustainable growth. The next chapters will build on this foundation, providing practical frameworks and tools to help you identify when a pivot is necessary and how to execute it successfully.

CHAPTER 2

IDENTIFYING THE NEED TO PIVOT:

Recognizing When Your Course Needs Correction

Every product journey starts with a vision and a clear path towards a desired destination. However, the business landscape is unpredictable, and the path is rarely as straightforward as planned. Market conditions change, customer preferences evolve, and competitors introduce new challenges. Recognizing when it's time to pivot can be the difference between success and failure. This chapter will provide frameworks and techniques to help you identify when a pivot is necessary.

Analyzing Market Shifts

The first step in recognizing the need for a pivot is to stay attuned to market shifts. Market dynamics can change rapidly due to various factors such as technological advancements, economic fluctuations, and regulatory changes. Regularly analyzing market trends can help you anticipate changes and make informed decisions about when to pivot.

One effective way to analyze market shifts is through competitive analysis. Keep a close eye on your competitors—both direct and indirect. Identify new entrants in the market, understand their strategies, and assess their impact on your business. Tools like SWOT (Strengths, Weaknesses, Opportunities, Threats) analysis can help you evaluate your competitive position and identify areas where a pivot might be necessary.

Another important aspect of market analysis is understanding your target audience. Conduct market research to gather insights into changing customer needs and preferences. Surveys, focus groups, and customer interviews are valuable methods for collecting qualitative data. Additionally, analyze demographic and psychographic data to identify emerging trends that could influence your product strategy.

Interpreting User Feedback

Customer feedback is a goldmine of information that can signal the need for a pivot. Regularly collecting and analyzing user feedback helps you stay connected with your audience and understand their evolving needs. There are several ways to gather user feedback, including surveys, reviews, social media interactions, and direct customer communication.

Pay close attention to recurring themes in user feedback. Are customers consistently mentioning certain pain points or requesting specific features? These patterns can indicate areas where your product may need to evolve. Negative feedback, in particular, can be a strong indicator that your current approach is not meeting customer expectations.

Utilize tools like Net Promoter Score (NPS) to gauge customer satisfaction and loyalty. A declining NPS score can be a red flag that your product is losing its appeal, signaling the need for a pivot. Additionally, monitoring customer support interactions can provide valuable insights into common issues and areas for improvement.

Evaluating Internal Performance Metrics

Internal performance metrics are another crucial aspect of identifying the need for a pivot. Key performance indicators (KPIs) such as sales figures, user engagement, customer acquisition cost, and churn rate can provide a clear picture of your product's health. A thorough analysis of these metrics can help you identify trends and anomalies that may warrant a strategic shift.

For instance, stagnant or declining sales figures may indicate that your product is not resonating with the market. Similarly, low user engagement or high churn rates could suggest that customers are not finding value in your product. Monitoring these metrics over time allows you to spot trends early and make proactive decisions.

Financial performance is also a critical consideration. Analyze your revenue streams, profit margins, and overall financial health. If you notice a decline in profitability or increasing costs without a corresponding increase in revenue, it might be time to reassess your business model and consider a pivot.

Frameworks for Recognizing the Need to Pivot

While the signs above offer valuable clues, a more structured approach can be helpful. Here are two frameworks to consider:

The BSQ Matrix: This framework focuses on three key questions:

- Better: Does your product offer a clear benefit or solve a significant problem for your target audience?
- Faster: Can your product deliver value to users more efficiently than competitors?
- Safer: Does your product offer a reliable and secure user experience?

If you answer "no" to any of these questions, it might be time to re-evaluate your strategy.

The HEART Framework: This framework focuses on user experience, prompting you to consider:

- Happiness: Does your product make users happy and fulfilled?
- Engagement: Does your product keep users engaged and coming back for more?

- Adoption: How easily can users adopt and integrate your product into their lives?
- Retention: Are users sticking with your product long-term, or are they churning at a high rate?

By analyzing your product through the lens of these frameworks, you can gain valuable insights into its strengths and weaknesses, ultimately helping you decide if a pivot is necessary.

Case Studies of Companies Recognizing the Need to Pivot

Twitter: Originally launched as Odeo, a platform for finding and subscribing to podcasts, Twitter pivoted to a microblogging platform after realizing the limited potential of its initial idea. The decision was driven by the founders' recognition of the growing popularity of social media and the unique value proposition of short, real-time updates.

BlackBerry: BlackBerry once dominated the smartphone market, known for its secure messaging and physical keyboard. However, they failed to recognize the shift towards larger touchscreens and a more app-centric user experience. Clinging to their original design ultimately led to their downfall.

Airbnb: Initially, Airbnb focused solely on connecting travellers with people who had spare rooms in their homes. However, they recognized the broader potential of the sharing economy and pivoted to include various accommodation types, from apartments to vacation rentals. This strategic shift fueled their remarkable growth and solidified their position as a travel industry leader.

Starbucks: Known today as a global coffeehouse chain, Starbucks initially sold espresso machines and coffee beans. The pivot to becoming a café was prompted by the founders' observations of coffee culture in Italy and the potential to create a unique customer experience centred around high-quality coffee beverages and a comfortable atmosphere.

Nintendo: Originally a playing card company, Nintendo pivoted several times, exploring different business ventures before finding success in the video game industry. The company's willingness to experiment and adapt to changing market conditions allowed it to become a dominant player in the gaming world.

These case studies illustrate the importance of staying vigilant, being open to change, and acting decisively when recognizing the need for a pivot. Each of these companies successfully navigated significant shifts in their strategies, ultimately leading to their long-term success.

Tools and Techniques for Continuous Market Analysis

To ensure you are always in tune with the market, it's essential to establish processes for continuous market analysis. Here are some tools and techniques to help you stay informed:

1. **SWOT Analysis:** Regularly conduct SWOT analyses to assess your strengths, weaknesses, opportunities, and threats. This helps you understand your competitive position and identify areas for potential pivots.
2. **PEST Analysis:** Analyze the external environment using PEST (Political, Economic, Social, and Technological) analysis. This framework helps you understand the macro-environmental factors that could impact your business.
3. **Porter's Five Forces:** Use Porter's Five Forces framework to analyze the competitive forces in your industry. This tool helps you assess the level of competition, the threat of new entrants, the bargaining power of suppliers and customers, and the threat of substitute products.
4. **Customer Journey Mapping:** Create detailed maps of your customers' journeys to identify pain points and areas for improvement. This technique helps you

understand the customer experience from start to finish and pinpoint opportunities for enhancement.

5. **Data Analytics Tools:** Leverage data analytics tools to gather and analyze quantitative data. Tools like Google Analytics, Mixpanel, and Tableau can provide valuable insights into user behaviour, engagement, and trends.

Recognizing the need for a pivot is a critical skill for product managers and business leaders. By staying attuned to market shifts, interpreting user feedback, and evaluating internal performance metrics, you can identify when a change is necessary. Continuous market analysis and the use of various tools and techniques will help you stay informed and make proactive decisions. The next chapter will build on this foundation, guiding you through the process of gathering intelligence and conducting user research to inform your pivot strategy.

CHAPTER 3

GATHERING INTELLIGENCE:

Analyzing Data and User Research for Informed Decisions

In the previous chapter, we explored the critical skill of recognizing the need to pivot. Now, we delve into the world of data analysis and user research, essential tools that equip you to gather valuable intelligence and make informed decisions about your pivot strategy. By combining the power of data with a deep understanding of your users, you can navigate the often murky waters of change with greater confidence and clarity.

The Power of Data Analysis

Data analysis is the process of collecting, cleaning, organizing, and interpreting data to extract meaningful insights. In product development, data analysis plays a crucial role in understanding your users, measuring product performance, and informing strategic decisions. There are two main types of data to consider:

1. **Quantitative Data:** This refers to measurable data points you can quantify and analyze statistically. Examples include sales figures, user engagement metrics (time spent on the app, number of features used), customer acquisition cost (CAC), and churn rate.
2. **Qualitative Data:** This encompasses non-numerical data that provides insights into user behaviour, motivations, and experiences. Examples include customer feedback from surveys and reviews, interview transcripts, and user testing observations.

A comprehensive understanding of your users and market requires analyzing both quantitative and qualitative data. Quantitative data provides the "what" – the measurable aspects of user behavior and product performance. Qualitative data provides the "why" – the underlying reasons behind the numbers, revealing user needs, frustrations, and motivations.

Data Analysis Tools and Techniques

A plethora of tools and techniques are available to help you harness the power of data analysis. Here are a few key players:

1. **Web Analytics Tools:** Tools like Google Analytics and Mixpanel offer valuable insights into user behaviour on your website or app. They track page views, user journeys, and conversion rates, and identify areas where users might be dropping off.
2. **Customer Relationship Management (CRM) Systems:** CRMs centralize customer data, providing insights into customer interactions and support tickets. Analyzing trends in customer inquiries can help identify recurring pain points.
3. **Data Visualization Tools:** Presenting data in an understandable and visually appealing way is crucial. Tools like Tableau and Power BI allow you to create charts, graphs, and dashboards that effectively communicate insights gleaned from data analysis.

It's important to remember that "garbage in, garbage out" applies to data analysis. Data hygiene is paramount, ensuring the data you collect is accurate, consistent, and complete. Regular data cleaning and validation processes are essential for reliable analysis.

User Research Methodologies

User research is the systematic process of understanding user needs, motivations, and behaviours. It helps you see your product through the eyes of your users and identify opportunities for improvement. Here are some core user research methodologies:

1. **Surveys:** Structured questionnaires allow you to gather quantitative data from a large sample size. Surveys are effective for gauging user sentiment, preferences, and usage patterns.
2. **Interviews:** In-depth conversations with users provide rich qualitative data. Open-ended questions help you understand user goals, challenges, and overall product experience.
3. **Usability Testing:** Observing users interacting with your product can help identify usability issues and areas for improvement. Watching how users navigate features

and complete tasks can reveal pain points or areas of confusion.

4. **A/B Testing:** Testing two different versions of a product feature or design determines which one performs better. A/B testing helps you optimize your product based on real user behaviour.

Choosing the right user research methodology depends on your specific research goals. Surveys are effective for gathering broad user opinions, while interviews provide deeper insights into individual experiences. Usability testing helps identify usability flaws, while A/B testing facilitates data-driven optimization.

Combining Data Analysis and User Research

The real magic happens when you combine data analysis and user research. Here's how:

1. **Uncover Hidden Patterns:** Data analysis might reveal a trend in user behaviour, but user research can help you understand the "why" behind it. For instance, quantitative data might show a decline in user engagement on a specific feature. User interviews can reveal that the feature is confusing or doesn't meet user needs.

2. **Validate Findings:** Quantitative data findings gain a stronger footing when validated by user research. For example, low customer satisfaction scores from surveys can be further explored through interviews to understand the root cause of dissatisfaction.
3. **Empathy is Key:** Data analysis provides valuable insights, but user research fosters empathy. By listening to your users and understanding their needs, you can develop a pivot strategy that truly resonates with them.

Examples of Data-Driven Pivots

Netflix: Data analysis revealed that a significant portion of users were abandoning their carts due to a complicated checkout process. User research through A/B testing of different checkout designs identified a simpler version that significantly reduced cart abandonment rates. This data-driven pivot improved user experience and boosted conversions.

Intuit: Initially focused on offering desktop tax software, Intuit noticed a shift in user behaviour towards mobile. By analyzing user data and conducting user research, they identified a growing demand for mobile tax solutions. This led them to pivot and develop the highly successful

TurboTax mobile app, catering to the evolving needs of their customers.

Data analysis and user research are powerful tools that empower you to gather valuable intelligence and inform your pivot strategy. By combining the power of data with a deep understanding of your users, you can make informed decisions, develop a pivot strategy with a higher chance of success, and ultimately navigate change with greater confidence. The next chapter will delve into the exciting world of crafting and implementing your pivot strategy, taking the insights gleaned from data and user research and translating them into a concrete plan for product transformation.

CHAPTER 4

CRAFTING AND IMPLEMENTING YOUR PIVOT STRATEGY

With a solid foundation of data analysis and user research, you are now ready to craft and implement your pivot strategy. This chapter will guide you through the steps to develop a clear and actionable pivot plan, ensuring alignment with your goals, resources, and team. We will explore how to set strategic objectives, engage stakeholders, and execute your pivot with precision and confidence.

Setting Strategic Objectives

The first step in crafting a pivot strategy is to set clear and measurable objectives. Your objectives should be aligned with the insights gathered from data analysis and user research, addressing the key issues identified and aiming to capitalize on new opportunities.

Define Your Goals: Start by defining what you want to achieve with your pivot. These goals could include increasing user engagement, expanding into a new market, improving product usability, or boosting revenue. Ensure your goals are specific, measurable, achievable, relevant, and time-bound (SMART).

Prioritize Objectives: Once you have defined your goals, prioritize them based on their impact and feasibility. Focus on the objectives that will deliver the most significant benefits and can be realistically achieved within your available resources and timeframe.

Align with Vision and Mission: Ensure that your pivot objectives align with your overall vision and mission. A pivot should not deviate from the core values and long-term goals of your organization. It should be a strategic adjustment that brings you closer to your ultimate aspirations.

Engaging Stakeholders

Successful pivots require the support and involvement of key stakeholders. Engaging stakeholders early in the process ensures alignment, builds trust, and fosters a sense of ownership. Here are some strategies for effective stakeholder engagement:

Identify Key Stakeholders: Identify all the stakeholders who will be impacted by the pivot, including team members, executives, investors, customers, and partners. Understand their interests, concerns, and expectations.

Communicate Transparently: Maintain open and honest communication with stakeholders throughout the pivot process. Clearly explain the reasons for the pivot, the expected benefits, and how it will be executed. Address any concerns and provide regular updates on progress.

Involve Stakeholders in Planning: Involve key stakeholders in the planning process to gather their insights and feedback. This collaborative approach ensures that diverse perspectives are considered and enhances the quality of your pivot strategy.

Build Consensus: Work towards building consensus among stakeholders. Use data and research findings to support your decisions and demonstrate the rationale behind your pivot. Address any disagreements constructively and strive for a shared understanding and commitment to the pivot.

Developing a Detailed Action Plan

A successful pivot requires a detailed action plan that outlines the steps, resources, and timelines necessary to achieve your objectives. Here's how to create an effective action plan:

First, break down your high-level objectives into smaller, manageable tasks. Define clear deliverables for each task and assign responsibilities to team members, ensuring everyone knows their specific roles and what is expected of them. This granular approach helps to manage the pivot process more efficiently and ensures accountability.

Next, set key milestones to track progress and ensure that the pivot stays on schedule. Milestones provide important checkpoints to assess whether the pivot is on track and allow for adjustments as needed. They also help maintain momentum and provide opportunities to celebrate small wins, keeping the team motivated.

Resource allocation is another critical aspect. Identify the resources required to execute the pivot, including budget, personnel, technology, and tools. Ensure that you have the necessary resources in place and allocate them effectively to support the pivot. Proper resource management helps avoid bottlenecks and ensures that all aspects of the pivot are adequately supported.

Develop contingency plans to anticipate potential challenges and risks that could arise during the pivot. By preparing for various scenarios, you can address these risks promptly and ensure that your team is prepared to handle any obstacles that may occur. This proactive approach helps mitigate risks and keeps the pivot process on track.

Finally, consider using agile project management methodologies, such as Scrum or Kanban, to manage the pivot process. Agile methodologies promote flexibility, collaboration, and iterative progress, making them well-suited for managing change. They enable teams to adapt quickly to new information and changing circumstances, ensuring that the pivot can be refined and optimized as needed.

By following these steps, you can create a comprehensive action plan that supports a smooth and successful pivot, positioning your product for future growth and success.

Executing the Pivot

With a detailed action plan in place, it's time to execute the pivot. Successful execution requires strong leadership, effective communication, and continuous monitoring. As a leader, set the tone for the pivot by demonstrating commitment, enthusiasm, and resilience. Inspire your team to embrace the change and work towards the common goals. Maintaining open and transparent communication is crucial. Provide regular updates on progress, celebrate successes, and address any issues promptly. Encourage feedback and ensure that team members feel heard and supported.

Continuous monitoring of the pivot's progress using key performance indicators (KPIs) and milestones is essential. Track metrics such as user engagement, customer feedback, sales figures, and project timelines to assess whether the pivot is achieving the desired outcomes. This data will help you make informed decisions and adjust strategies as needed. Flexibility is crucial during a pivot, as unforeseen challenges and opportunities may arise. Stay agile and be prepared to adapt your strategy based on ongoing insights and feedback.

Support your team throughout the process by providing the necessary resources and addressing any concerns. Offer training and resources to help them navigate the pivot successfully. Recognize their efforts and achievements to maintain morale and motivation. This combination of strong leadership, open communication, continuous monitoring, flexibility, and team support will ensure the pivot is executed smoothly and effectively, turning potential setbacks into opportunities for growth and success. By fostering a supportive environment and being responsive to both data and team feedback, you can navigate the complexities of a pivot with confidence and achieve your strategic objectives.

Case Studies of Some Successful Pivots

Twitter: Originally launched as Odeo, a platform for finding and subscribing to podcasts, Twitter pivoted to a microblogging platform after realizing the limited potential of its initial idea. This decision was driven by the founders' recognition of the growing popularity of social media and the unique value proposition of short, real-time updates. The pivot transformed Twitter into a leading social media platform.

Instagram: Initially launched as a photo-sharing app called Burbn, Instagram pivoted to focus on mobile photo sharing with a user-friendly interface and emphasis on filters. This strategic shift propelled them to become a dominant social media platform. The pivot was driven by user feedback that highlighted the popularity of photo-sharing features, leading to a streamlined and focused product offering.

Slack: Developed initially as a game creation tool called Glitch, Slack pivoted to a team communication platform after recognizing the growing need for real-time collaboration tools in the workplace. This focus on a specific market need fueled their remarkable growth and established them as a leader in the communication software space. The pivot was guided by internal insights and a clear understanding of the market's evolving needs.

Netflix: Netflix started as a DVD rental-by-mail service but pivoted to streaming services as they foresaw the shift in consumer preferences towards on-demand content. This strategic pivot was driven by market analysis and the recognition of the potential for a digital streaming platform. Today, Netflix is a leading global entertainment service, continually adapting to changes in technology and consumer behavior.

Crafting and implementing a pivot strategy is a complex but rewarding process. By setting clear objectives, engaging stakeholders, developing a detailed action plan, and executing with precision, you can navigate the pivot successfully. Continuous monitoring and flexibility are key to ensuring that the pivot achieves its intended goals. The next chapter will explore how to measure the success of your pivot and learn from the experience to foster continuous improvement and growth.

CHAPTER 5

STAKEHOLDER MANAGEMENT IN A CHANGING LANDSCAPE

Congratulations! You've successfully navigated the pivot, implementing a strategic shift to address market demands and user needs. But the journey doesn't end here. To ensure long-term success, you need to maintain momentum and keep your product relevant. This chapter will guide you on two crucial, interconnected aspects: Continuous Improvement and Agility, and Stakeholder Management. Regularly monitor key metrics such as user engagement, customer sentiment, and sales figures. This data, along with ongoing feedback, will inform adjustments to your product and strategy. Be prepared to stay agile and adapt to unforeseen challenges and opportunities. Successful pivots rely heavily on effective stakeholder management. Stakeholders, including team members, investors, customers, and partners, all play a critical role. This chapter will explore strategies for managing expectations by communicating openly and transparently throughout the process, setting realistic goals and timelines; alignment across departments to ensure everyone understands the new direction and how their role contributes to success; and garnering support by fostering open communication to address concerns, providing training as needed, and celebrating milestones together. By focusing on both continuous improvement and effective stakeholder management, you can ensure your product stays on course for long-term success after the pivot.

Focus on Continuous Improvement and Effective Stakeholder Management

A successful pivot doesn't signify the end of the product development cycle. Embrace a culture of continuous improvement while effectively managing key stakeholders. This dual focus ensures that your product evolves in line with user expectations and maintains stakeholder support. Here are some key strategies:

Iterative Development and Communication:

Utilize iterative development methodologies like Agile to continuously release new features and improvements based on user feedback and data analysis. This approach allows for flexibility and rapid response to user needs and market changes. Internally, host kickoff meetings to announce the pivot, explain the rationale behind it, and outline expected outcomes. Providing regular updates through team meetings, emails, and internal newsletters helps maintain alignment and morale.

A/B Testing and Feedback Loops:

Continue A/B testing different features and functionalities to optimize user engagement and conversion. Testing variations helps identify what works best and guides data-driven decision-making. Establish channels for feedback where team members can share their thoughts, concerns, and suggestions, fostering a sense of inclusion and collaboration. Additionally, robust user feedback loops should be established to gather ongoing user input and identify areas for further improvement.

Metrics that Matter:

Track user acquisition rates and churn rates to measure the effectiveness of your pivot in attracting and retaining users. High retention rates indicate that users find value in the new product direction. Monitor metrics like time spent on the app, feature usage, and user activity to understand user engagement with the new product direction. High engagement levels typically correlate with user satisfaction and loyalty. Utilize tools like Net Promoter Score (NPS) to track customer satisfaction and identify areas for further improvement. High NPS scores indicate strong user advocacy and satisfaction.

Stakeholder Management:

Identify all individuals and groups impacted by the pivot, categorizing them into internal stakeholders (team members, department heads, and executives) and external stakeholders (investors, customers, partners, suppliers, and industry influencers). Understanding their interests and concerns is crucial for developing an effective engagement strategy. For external communication, hold briefings with investors to explain the pivot, provide data-driven insights supporting the change, and outline expected benefits. Transparency with investors helps maintain their confidence and support. Communicate with customers about the changes they can expect and how the pivot will benefit them. Use emails, social media, and customer support channels to keep them informed and engaged. Additionally, meet with key partners to explain how the pivot will impact the partnership and explore ways to collaborate more effectively during the transition.

By integrating continuous improvement with effective stakeholder management, you can ensure a smooth transition during a pivot while enhancing user experience and maintaining strong support from all involved parties.

Staying Agile, Adapting to Change, and Aligning Stakeholders

The business landscape is constantly evolving, and maintaining an agile mindset while ensuring cross-departmental alignment is crucial for a successful pivot. Here are strategies to stay ahead of the curve and align stakeholders across departments.

Staying Agile and Adapting to Change

To navigate the ever-changing business environment, it is essential to stay agile and be prepared to adapt your product strategy as needed. One key approach is market monitoring. Continuously monitor market trends and competitor activity to identify new opportunities and threats. Staying informed allows you to anticipate changes and adjust your strategy proactively. Embracing innovation is another vital aspect. Foster a culture of innovation within your team, encouraging experimentation and exploration of new technologies and ideas. Innovation drives growth and keeps your product competitive. Additionally, learning from others is beneficial. Learn from the successes and failures of other companies in your industry. Identify best practices and adapt them to your own context. This approach helps you avoid common pitfalls and leverage proven strategies.

Aligning Stakeholders across Departments

Cross-departmental alignment is crucial for a seamless pivot. Clearly articulate a unified vision and goals for the pivot, ensuring that all departments understand the overarching objectives and how their contributions fit into the bigger picture. Collaborative planning is essential; involve representatives from different departments in the planning process. This collaborative approach ensures that diverse perspectives are considered and helps identify potential challenges early on. Regular interdepartmental meetings are also important. Schedule these meetings to discuss progress, share insights, and address any issues that arise. These meetings foster collaboration and ensure that everyone is working towards the same goals.

Garnering Support for the New Direction

Building support for the pivot among stakeholders is essential for its success. Use data and research findings to justify the pivot. Presenting clear evidence of market shifts, user needs, and performance metrics helps stakeholders understand the rationale behind the change. Clearly communicate the benefits of the pivot to each stakeholder group, whether it's improved user experience, increased market opportunities, or long-term growth potential. Stakeholders need to see how the pivot will positively impact them. Be proactive in addressing any concerns or objections that stakeholders may have. Provide detailed explanations and be open to feedback. Addressing concerns head-on builds trust and credibility. Finally, celebrate key milestones and successes throughout the pivot process. Recognizing and rewarding achievements helps maintain momentum and keeps stakeholders motivated and engaged. By staying agile, adapting to change, and ensuring cross-departmental alignment, you can successfully navigate a pivot while maintaining strong support from all involved parties

Case Studies of Some Organization Sustaining Momentum

Spotify: Spotify's success lies in its constant evolution. They pivoted from a freemium model with limited features to a subscription-based model offering extensive music libraries and exclusive podcasts. Additionally, they continuously adapt their platform, integrating new features like personalized playlists and social sharing options. Spotify's commitment to continuous improvement and innovation has kept them at the forefront of the music streaming industry. Their ability to leverage data analytics to personalize user experiences and their focus on mobile optimization have been key drivers of their sustained success.

Amazon: Amazon's relentless focus on customer satisfaction and continuous improvement has fueled their long-term success. They constantly add new product categories, refine their user experience, and leverage data analysis to personalize product recommendations for each user.

Amazon's ability to adapt to market trends and user needs has solidified its position as a global e-commerce leader. Their innovation in logistics, such as the development of the Prime delivery service, and their expansion into cloud computing with AWS are prime examples of their adaptive strategy.

Netflix: Netflix started as a DVD rental-by-mail service but pivoted to streaming services as they foresaw the shift in consumer preferences towards on-demand content. This strategic pivot was driven by market analysis and the recognition of the potential for a digital streaming platform. Today, Netflix is a leading global entertainment service, continually adapting to changes in technology and consumer behavior. Their investment in original content and their use of sophisticated algorithms to recommend shows and movies to users have been pivotal to their growth and user retention.

Maintaining momentum after a pivot requires dedication, agility, and a commitment to continuous improvement. By consistently monitoring key metrics, embracing user feedback, and staying adaptable in a dynamic market, you can ensure your product thrives in the long run. Remember, the pivot is just one chapter in your product's story. By fostering a culture of innovation and user-centricity, you can write a story of sustained success for your product. The journey post-pivot involves constantly evolving your product to meet user needs, leveraging data to inform decisions, and staying agile to adapt to new challenges and opportunities. Whether through iterative development, robust feedback loops, or embracing innovation, the key is to remain focused on providing value to your users. By doing so, you not only maintain the momentum of your pivot but also build a resilient product that can withstand the test of time. Through the examples of Spotify, Amazon, and Netflix, it is evident that continuous evolution, a keen focus on customer satisfaction, and the ability to adapt to market changes are crucial for sustained success. Embrace these principles, and you will be well on your way to keeping your product on course for long-term growth and relevance.

CHAPTER 6

EFFECTIVE COMMUNICATION STRATEGIES FOR LEADING THROUGH CHANGE

In the world of product development, change is inevitable. Whether you're pivoting your product, entering a new market, or launching a new feature, effective communication is critical to ensure everyone remains aligned, motivated, and focused on the same goals. This chapter will delve into the strategies for effective communication that will help you lead your team through change with clarity and purpose.

The Importance of Communication in Change Management

Effective communication during periods of change is essential for several reasons. Firstly, it provides clarity, helping everyone understand the reasons behind the change, the benefits it will bring, and their role in the process. When communication is clear and consistent, it ensures alignment, meaning that efforts are coordinated and resources are used efficiently. Additionally, transparent communication can help maintain morale and keep the team motivated, even when facing uncertainty. Finally, open and honest communication builds trust between leadership and team members, fostering a positive work environment.

Crafting Your Communication Strategy

To lead your team through change effectively, you need a well-thought-out communication strategy. The first step is to define your message. Ensure that your message is clear and consistent across all channels, avoiding jargon and keeping the language simple and straightforward. Clearly articulate the purpose of the change and the vision for the future, explaining how the change aligns with the company's overall goals and values. Highlight the benefits of the change for the company, the team, and the customers, and be honest about the potential challenges and how they will be addressed.

Choosing the right channels for communication is equally important. Host regular meetings to discuss the change, provide updates, and address any questions or concerns. These meetings should be inclusive and interactive. Written communication, such as emails and newsletters, can provide detailed information and updates, ensuring everyone has a reference point they can revisit. Utilize your company's intranet or collaboration tools, like Slack or Microsoft Teams, to share information and foster ongoing dialogue.

Tailoring your communication to your audience is crucial. Customize your messages for different stakeholder groups. Investors, employees, and customers may need different types of information. Provide channels for feedback and encourage team members to voice their concerns and suggestions. This can be through surveys, suggestion boxes, or direct conversations, fostering a sense of inclusion and collaboration.

Strategies for Leading through Change

Leading through change requires more than just disseminating information. It involves demonstrating commitment, maintaining a positive attitude, and actively engaging with your team. As a leader, you should show your commitment to the change by being actively involved and engaged in the process. Your demeanor can significantly influence your team's morale and attitude toward the change, so maintaining a positive and resilient attitude is essential.

Fostering open communication is also vital. Be transparent about the progress, successes, and challenges of the change process. Regularly update the team and be honest about any setbacks. Listen to your team's concerns and feedback, acknowledging their feelings and providing reassurance where possible. Supporting your team through resources and training ensures they have the necessary tools to adapt to the change. Offering support through workshops, training sessions, and one-on-one coaching can be incredibly beneficial. Recognize and reward the efforts and achievements of your team members, as celebrating small wins can boost morale and motivation.

Maintaining flexibility is another key strategy. Be prepared to adjust your plans based on feedback and new information. Show flexibility in your approach and be willing to make necessary changes to the strategy. Having contingency plans in place to address potential challenges ensures that the team is prepared for unexpected obstacles and can adapt quickly.

Case Studies: Effective Communication in Change Management

When Microsoft decided to pivot from a software-focused company to a cloud-first organization, their communication strategy was pivotal to the transition's success. They maintained transparency with their employees about the reasons for the shift and the benefits it would bring. Regular updates, training sessions, and open forums for discussion helped align the entire organization with the new direction. Similarly, Adobe's transition from a traditional software licensing model to a subscription-based service (Adobe Creative Cloud) required clear and consistent communication. They engaged with their customers to explain the benefits of the subscription model, provided comprehensive training to their internal teams, and ensured that stakeholders were regularly updated on the progress of the transition. This approach helped Adobe manage the change smoothly and maintain customer trust.

Effective communication is the cornerstone of leading through change. By defining a clear message, choosing the right communication channels, tailoring your communication to different audiences, and employing strategies to lead effectively, you can ensure that your team remains aligned, motivated, and ready to embrace the change. Remember, successful change management relies on transparency, active listening, and continuous support. The next chapter will delve into the strategies for prioritizing and allocating resources during a pivot, ensuring that your team remains focused on the most critical elements for success.

CHAPTER 7

PRIORITIZATION AND RESOURCE ALLOCATION:

Making Tough Choices during a Pivot

Pivoting a product requires making tough choices about where to focus efforts and resources. Ensuring that your team is working on the most critical elements can determine the success of your pivot. This chapter explores strategies for prioritizing tasks and allocating resources effectively, helping you navigate the complexities of change while maintaining focus and efficiency.

The Importance of Prioritization

When undertaking a pivot, it's essential to prioritize tasks to ensure that the most critical aspects of the product receive the necessary attention. Prioritization helps in focusing efforts on high-impact areas, managing time and resources efficiently, and avoiding the pitfalls of spreading your team too thin. By determining which tasks will deliver the most significant benefits and align with your strategic goals, you can direct your team's efforts where they will have the most impact.

Frameworks for Prioritization

Several frameworks can assist in the prioritization process, each offering a structured approach to evaluating tasks and making informed decisions. One widely used framework is the Eisenhower Matrix, which helps prioritize tasks based on their urgency and importance. Tasks are categorized into four quadrants: urgent and important (tasks that need immediate attention and have a significant impact), not urgent but important (tasks that are important but can be scheduled for later), urgent but not important (tasks that need to be addressed quickly but have less impact), and not urgent and not important (tasks that can be delegated or eliminated). This matrix aids in focusing on high-priority tasks while managing or delegating lower-priority ones.

Another useful framework is the MoSCoW method, which categorizes tasks into four groups: must-have (essential tasks critical to the success of the pivot), should-have (important tasks that should be included if possible), could-have (desirable tasks that can be deferred if time and resources permit), and won't-have (non-essential tasks that can be excluded for now). This method helps prioritize tasks based on their necessity and impact on the project.

The RICE scoring model is also effective, evaluating tasks based on four factors: reach (the number of people the task will impact), impact (the degree of impact the task will have on the project or product), confidence (the level of confidence in the estimates and assumptions), and effort (the amount of effort required to complete the task). Each factor is scored, and the total score helps prioritize tasks based on their overall potential impact and feasibility.

Resource Allocation Strategies

Effective resource allocation ensures that the right people, budget, and tools are dedicated to the most critical tasks. Here are some strategies for allocating resources during a pivot:

Start by assessing the availability of resources, including budget, personnel, technology, and tools. Understanding the current resource pool helps in making informed decisions about allocation and identifying any gaps that need to be addressed. Once resource availability is clear, allocate resources based on the prioritization framework you've chosen. Ensure that high-priority tasks receive sufficient resources to be completed efficiently. This alignment helps in maximizing the impact of your efforts and avoiding resource wastage.

Maintain flexibility in resource allocation to adapt to changes and new information. Be prepared to reallocate resources as needed based on ongoing assessments and feedback. This adaptability ensures that resources are used effectively and can be redirected to address emerging challenges or opportunities. Additionally, leverage cross-functional teams to bring diverse skills and perspectives to critical tasks. This approach promotes collaboration, innovation, and efficient problem-solving. Cross-functional teams can tackle complex tasks more effectively by combining expertise from different areas.

Continuously monitor the allocation of resources and the progress of tasks. Regularly review the effectiveness of resource allocation and make adjustments as necessary. This ongoing assessment helps in optimizing resource use and ensuring that priorities remain aligned with strategic goals.

Implementing Agile Methodologies

Agile methodologies, such as Scrum and Kanban, can be highly effective in managing prioritization and resource allocation during a pivot. These methodologies promote flexibility, collaboration, and iterative progress, making them well-suited for navigating change.

Scrum

Scrum involves breaking down the project into smaller, manageable sprints. Each sprint focuses on a set of prioritized tasks, allowing the team to work on high-impact areas and deliver incremental improvements. Regular sprint reviews and retrospectives help in assessing progress and making necessary adjustments. By breaking down the project into these sprints, Scrum facilitates a focused approach to high-priority tasks, ensuring that the most critical aspects of the pivot are addressed efficiently and effectively. This iterative process allows for continuous improvement and adaptability, crucial for a successful pivot.

Kanban

Kanban emphasizes visualizing the workflow and managing work in progress. Tasks are represented on a Kanban board, allowing the team to see the status of each task and identify bottlenecks. This method helps in maintaining a steady flow of work and ensuring that resources are allocated efficiently. By visualizing the entire workflow, Kanban makes it easier to manage and optimize the process, ensuring that tasks move smoothly from one stage to the next. This transparency helps in quickly identifying and addressing any issues that may arise, promoting a more efficient allocation of resources and enhancing overall productivity.

Implementing these Agile methodologies can significantly enhance the management of prioritization and resource allocation during a pivot. Scrum's focus on iterative progress and continuous feedback, combined with Kanban's visualization of the workflow, provides a comprehensive approach to navigating the complexities of change. This adaptability and focus on collaboration ensure that the pivot is not only managed effectively but also positioned for success.

Case Studies: Effective Prioritization and Resource Allocation.

Let me tell you about a couple of great examples of how effective prioritization and resource allocation can drive success during a pivot. Take Slack, for instance. It started as a game creation tool called Glitch, but when they decided to pivot to a team communication platform, they had to carefully prioritize their tasks and allocate their resources. They focused on developing essential communication features and integrating feedback from early users. By concentrating their resources on high-impact tasks, Slack transformed into the leading collaboration tool we know today.

Another fascinating example is Airbnb. Originally, Airbnb was a platform for renting air mattresses, but they pivoted to become a comprehensive accommodation booking service. To achieve this, they prioritized enhancing the user experience and building trust with their users. They allocated resources to improving the booking process, implementing a secure payment system, and expanding their range of available accommodations. This strategic focus on critical elements allowed Airbnb to scale rapidly and establish itself as a trusted platform.

Prioritization and resource allocation are vital for a successful pivot. By using structured frameworks to evaluate tasks and making informed decisions about where to allocate resources, you can ensure your team focuses on the most critical elements. Implementing agile methodologies further enhances flexibility and efficiency, allowing you to adapt to changes and optimize resource use. Next, we'll explore the art of communication and how to effectively convey your pivot to the market, ensuring that your new direction resonates with your target audience.

CHAPTER 8

PRODUCT REPOSITIONING:

Messaging Your Pivot to the Market

Repositioning your product after a pivot is crucial to ensuring that your new direction resonates with your target audience. Effective messaging and marketing strategies are essential to communicate the value of your product and align with the market's evolving needs. This chapter will explore how to craft compelling messaging and adjust your marketing efforts to support your new product direction.

Understanding Your New Market Position

Repositioning your product effectively starts with a clear understanding of your new market position. This process involves identifying your target audience, analyzing your competitors, and defining your unique value proposition. First, re-evaluate your target audience to ensure that your product aligns with their needs and preferences. Conducting thorough market research will provide insights into their demographics, behaviors, and pain points. Understanding your audience helps you tailor your messaging to address their specific needs, making your product more appealing and relevant to them. Next, analyze your competitors to identify gaps in the market and opportunities for differentiation. By understanding what your competitors offer and how they position themselves, you can craft a unique value proposition that sets your product apart. This analysis is crucial for finding ways to stand out in a crowded market. Finally, define your unique value proposition (UVP). Your UVP is the cornerstone of your product messaging, clearly articulating what makes your product different and why customers should choose it over competitors. It should address the specific needs and pain points of your target audience while highlighting the benefits and value your product delivers. A strong UVP ensures that your product resonates with potential customers and stands out in the marketplace.

Crafting Compelling Messaging

Once you have a clear understanding of your new market position, it's time to craft compelling messaging that communicates the value of your product. Here are some key elements to consider:

First, your messaging should be clear, concise, and easy to understand. Avoid jargon and complex language that might confuse your audience. Instead, focus on the key benefits and value your product offers. Clear messaging ensures that your audience quickly grasps the advantages of your product without getting lost in unnecessary details.

Next, aim to connect with your audience on an emotional level by addressing their pain points and desires. Use storytelling techniques to create a narrative that resonates with your audience and highlights how your product can improve their lives. Emotional appeal makes your messaging more engaging and memorable, helping potential customers feel a personal connection to your product.

Maintaining a consistent brand voice across all communication channels is also crucial. Your brand voice should reflect your company's values and personality, creating a cohesive and recognizable identity. Consistency in tone and style helps build trust and reinforces your brand's presence in the market.

Lastly, include clear calls to action (CTAs) that guide your audience towards the desired outcome, whether it's signing up for a newsletter, requesting a demo, or making a purchase. Your CTAs should be specific, actionable, and aligned with your overall marketing goals. Effective CTAs encourage your audience to take the next step and engage more deeply with your product.

By incorporating these elements, you can craft compelling messaging that effectively communicates your product's value, resonates with your audience, and drives engagement and conversion.

Adjusting Your Marketing Strategy

Repositioning your product requires adjustments to your marketing strategy to ensure your new messaging reaches the right audience through the right channels. Here are some key steps to take:

First, revamp your website and digital presence. Your website is often the first point of contact for potential customers, so it's essential to update it to reflect your new product positioning. Ensure that your website content, design, and user experience align with your new messaging. Additionally, optimize your website for search engines (SEO) to increase visibility and attract organic traffic. A well-optimized website helps potential customers find you more easily and engage with your updated brand message.

Next, leverage content marketing as a powerful tool for educating your audience and building trust. Create high-quality content that addresses the needs and pain points of your target audience. This can include blog posts, whitepapers, case studies, videos, and webinars. Share your content through your website, social media channels, and email campaigns. Providing valuable content positions you as a thought leader and helps build a strong relationship with your audience.

Utilize social media platforms as effective channels for reaching and engaging with your audience. Update your social media profiles to reflect your new product positioning and share relevant content that resonates with your audience. Use social media advertising to target specific demographics and amplify your reach. Engaging consistently on social media helps maintain a vibrant presence and keeps your audience informed about your product.

Engage with influencers to increase brand awareness and credibility. Partnering with influencers in your industry can help you reach a wider audience and build trust. Identify influencers who align with your brand values and have a strong following among your target audience. Collaborate with them to create authentic and engaging content that promotes your product. Influencers can effectively bridge the gap between your brand and potential customers.

Email marketing campaigns are a cost-effective way to nurture leads and maintain relationships with existing customers. Update your email marketing campaigns to reflect your new product positioning and provide valuable content that addresses the needs of your audience. Personalize your emails to increase engagement and drive conversions. Email marketing allows for direct communication with your audience, keeping them engaged and informed about your product updates.

Lastly, monitor and measure the results of your marketing efforts to ensure they are effective in achieving your goals. Use analytics tools to track key performance indicators (KPIs) such as website traffic, social media engagement, email open rates, and conversion rates. Use this data to make informed decisions and optimize your marketing strategy. Regular monitoring and analysis help you understand what's working and where adjustments are needed, ensuring your marketing efforts remain effective and aligned with your goals.

Case Studies: Successful Product Repositioning.

Let's talk about a couple of notable examples of successful product repositioning that highlight the power of strategic messaging and marketing.

Apple has successfully repositioned its products multiple times over the years, with the iPhone being a prime example. Initially marketed as a revolutionary communication device, the iPhone has evolved into a versatile tool for communication, entertainment, photography, and more. Apple's consistent messaging, emotional appeal, and innovative marketing campaigns have helped maintain its position as a market leader. Their ability to adapt and highlight the multifaceted use of the iPhone has kept it relevant and desirable across different market segments.

Old Spice is another great example. They repositioned themselves from a brand associated with older generations to one that appeals to younger audiences. Through humorous and memorable advertising campaigns, Old Spice reinvented its image and attracted a new customer base. Their use of social media and influencer partnerships further amplified their reach and success. This repositioning has transformed Old Spice into a contemporary and relatable brand for a new generation.

Repositioning your product after a pivot requires a strategic approach to messaging and marketing. By understanding your new market position, crafting compelling messaging, and adjusting your marketing strategy, you can effectively communicate the value of your product and resonate with your target audience. Remember, successful product repositioning relies on clear communication, emotional appeal, consistent branding, and continuous optimization.

In the next chapter, we'll explore metrics and measuring success, providing you with the tools to track the impact of your pivot and refine your strategy for long-term growth. This will equip you with the insights needed to ensure your repositioning efforts lead to sustained success.

CHAPTER 9

METRICS AND MEASURING SUCCESS:

Tracking the Impact of Your Pivot

After a successful pivot, it is crucial to measure the impact of the changes to ensure that your new strategy is delivering the desired outcomes. Tracking the right metrics allows you to assess the effectiveness of your pivot, identify areas for improvement, and make data-driven decisions to sustain growth. This chapter will explore key performance indicators (KPIs) and measurement techniques to help you evaluate the success of your pivot.

Defining Success Metrics

The first step in measuring success is defining the metrics that align with your strategic goals. These metrics should be specific, measurable, and relevant to the objectives of your pivot. Here are some essential metrics to consider:

User Acquisition and Retention

Tracking user acquisition and retention rates provides insights into the effectiveness of your marketing efforts and the overall appeal of your product. Key metrics include Customer Acquisition Cost (CAC), which measures the total cost of acquiring a new customer, including marketing and sales expenses. The Customer Retention Rate indicates the percentage of customers who continue to use your product over a specific period, while the Churn Rate measures the percentage of customers who stop using your product during a given timeframe.

User Engagement

Engagement metrics help you understand how users interact with your product and identify areas for improvement. Key metrics include Daily Active Users (DAU) and Monthly Active Users (MAU), which track the number of unique users who engage with your product daily and monthly. Average Session Duration measures the average amount of time users spend on your product during each session, and Feature Usage indicates the frequency and popularity of specific features within your product.

Revenue and Profitability

Revenue metrics are critical for assessing the financial success of your pivot. Monthly Recurring Revenue (MRR) tracks the total revenue generated from subscription-based products on a monthly basis. Average Revenue Per User (ARPU) measures the average revenue generated per user over a specific period, while Customer Lifetime Value (CLTV) calculates the total revenue a customer is expected to generate over their lifetime with your product.

Customer Satisfaction

Measuring customer satisfaction provides insights into how well your product meets user needs. Net Promoter Score (NPS) gauges customer loyalty and the likelihood to recommend your product to others. Customer Satisfaction Score (CSAT) measures customer satisfaction with specific interactions or the overall experience, while Customer Effort

Score (CES) assesses how easy it is for customers to use your product and resolve issues.

Product Performance

Product performance metrics help you ensure that your product functions reliably and efficiently. Key metrics include Load Times, which measure the average time it takes for your product to load, Crash Rates that track the frequency of product crashes or technical issues, and Error Rates, indicating the number of errors encountered by users during product use.

By defining and tracking these success metrics, you can gain a comprehensive understanding of your product's performance and the effectiveness of your pivot. This data will inform your decisions, helping you refine your strategy and achieve long-term growth.

Implementing Measurement Techniques

To effectively track these metrics, you need robust measurement techniques and tools. Here are some strategies for implementing these techniques:

Data Collection Tools

Utilize data collection tools to gather accurate and comprehensive data on user behavior, product performance, and financial metrics. Tools such as Google Analytics, Mixpanel, and Amplitude are excellent for tracking user interactions and engagement. CRM systems like Salesforce can provide insights into customer acquisition and retention, while financial software like QuickBooks can help monitor revenue and profitability. These tools collectively enable you to have a detailed understanding of your key performance indicators.

A/B Testing

A/B testing allows you to compare different versions of your product or marketing strategies to determine which performs better. By testing variations, you can optimize user experience and make data-driven decisions. Use A/B testing tools like Optimizely or VWO to conduct experiments and analyze results. This approach helps in fine-tuning aspects of your product or strategy to better meet user needs and improve overall performance.

Surveys and Feedback

Collecting direct feedback from users through surveys and feedback forms provides valuable qualitative data. Tools like SurveyMonkey and Typeform can help you create and distribute surveys to gather insights into customer satisfaction, feature preferences, and overall experience. Engaging with your users directly allows you to understand their needs and expectations more deeply, guiding improvements and fostering a customer-centric approach.

Dashboards and Reporting

Creating dashboards and reports helps you visualize and analyze data effectively. Use tools like Tableau, Power BI, or Google Data Studio to create custom dashboards that track key metrics and provide real-time insights. Regularly reviewing these reports allows you to monitor progress, identify trends, and make informed decisions. Dashboards provide a clear, visual representation of your data, making it easier to understand and act upon.

By implementing these measurement techniques, you can systematically track and analyze your key metrics, enabling you to make informed decisions and optimize your strategies for long-term success.

Analyzing and Interpreting Data

Once you have collected the data, the next step is to analyze and interpret it to gain actionable insights. Here are some techniques for effective data analysis:

Trend Analysis

Analyzing trends over time helps you understand how your metrics are evolving and identify patterns. Look for trends in user acquisition, engagement, revenue, and satisfaction to assess the impact of your pivot. By comparing historical data before and after the pivot, you can gauge the effectiveness of your new strategies and identify areas that need further improvement.

Segmentation

Segmenting your data allows you to analyze specific groups of users based on demographics, behavior, or other criteria. This helps you identify which segments are most affected by the pivot and tailor your strategies accordingly. For example, segmenting users by age, location, or usage frequency can reveal insights into how different groups interact with your product, enabling you to customize your approach for each segment.

Correlation Analysis

Correlation analysis helps you identify relationships between different metrics. For instance, you might analyze the correlation between customer satisfaction scores and retention rates to understand how user experience impacts loyalty. Identifying these correlations can help you pinpoint areas for improvement and prioritize efforts that will have the most significant impact on your key metrics.

Benchmarking

Comparing your performance against industry benchmarks or competitors provides context for your metrics. Benchmarking helps you set realistic goals and measure your progress relative to others in your industry. This can highlight areas where you excel and those that need improvement. Understanding where you stand in comparison to industry standards can guide your strategic decisions and ensure you remain competitive.

By applying these techniques, you can turn raw data into valuable insights that drive informed decision-making and strategic planning. This analytical approach ensures that your efforts are targeted, effective, and aligned with your overall business goals.

Case Studies: Measuring Success after a Pivot.

Understanding how to measure success after a pivot is essential, and looking at successful examples can provide valuable insights. Take Slack, for instance. After pivoting from a game development company to a team communication platform, Slack meticulously tracked metrics such as user acquisition, engagement, and retention. By continuously analyzing data, they identified the features that drove the most value and optimized their product accordingly. This data-driven approach was crucial to their rapid growth and widespread adoption.

Similarly, Dropbox's pivot from a consumer-focused file storage service to a business-oriented collaboration platform required careful measurement of business user metrics. They tracked metrics such as business account sign-ups, active users, and integration usage to ensure their new strategy was successful. By focusing on data, Dropbox was able to refine their product and grow their enterprise customer base significantly.

Measuring the success of your pivot is crucial for ensuring that your new strategy is delivering the desired outcomes. By defining and tracking the right metrics, implementing robust measurement techniques, and analyzing the data effectively, you can make informed decisions to sustain growth and improve your product. Remember, continuous measurement and optimization are key to long-term success.

The next chapter will explore how to foster a culture of experimentation and continuous learning, ensuring that your team remains innovative and adaptable in a constantly changing market. This approach will help your organization stay ahead of the curve and consistently deliver value to your customers.

CHAPTER 10

LEARNING FROM THE PIVOT:

Fostering a Culture of Experimentation and Continuous Learning

A successful pivot is not the end of the journey; it is a step towards continuous growth and improvement. Fostering a culture of experimentation and continuous learning is essential to ensure that your team remains innovative and adaptable. This chapter will explore how to create an environment that encourages experimentation, embraces failure as a learning opportunity, and continuously refines your product based on new insights.

Embracing a Growth Mindset

A growth mindset is the foundation of a culture of experimentation and continuous learning. It involves believing that abilities and intelligence can be developed through dedication and hard work. Here are key aspects to consider:

Encourage Curiosity

Foster an environment where team members are encouraged to ask questions, explore new ideas, and challenge the status quo. Curiosity drives innovation and helps identify new opportunities for improvement. When team members feel safe to express their thoughts and ideas, they are more likely to contribute creative solutions and explore unconventional approaches.

Promote Learning and Development

Invest in the continuous learning and development of your team. Provide access to training programs, workshops, conferences, and online courses. Encourage team members to stay updated with industry trends and best practices. By prioritizing education, you empower your team with the knowledge and skills they need to innovate and adapt to new challenges.

Recognize and Reward Effort

Acknowledge and reward the efforts of team members who demonstrate a growth mindset. Celebrate both successes and failures as valuable learning experiences. Recognizing effort reinforces the importance of continuous improvement and motivates the team to keep pushing boundaries. When failures are seen as stepping stones to success, team members are more likely to take calculated risks and pursue ambitious goals.

By fostering a culture that values curiosity, learning, and recognition, you create an environment where experimentation and continuous improvement thrive. This culture not only supports the current pivot but also prepares your team to navigate future changes and challenges with confidence and resilience.

Encouraging Experimentation

Experimentation is at the heart of innovation. By testing new ideas and approaches, you can discover what works best and make data-driven decisions. Here are some strategies to encourage experimentation:

Create a Safe Environment

Establish a safe environment where team members feel comfortable taking risks and trying new things without fear of failure. Encourage open communication and provide support when experiments don't go as planned. When people know they won't be penalized for failed attempts, they are more likely to explore bold and innovative ideas.

Implement Agile Methodologies

Agile methodologies, such as Scrum and Kanban, promote iterative development and continuous experimentation. By working in short sprints and regularly reviewing progress, teams can quickly test new ideas, gather feedback, and make improvements. This approach allows for rapid adaptation and refinement, essential for navigating the uncertainties that come with innovation.

Use A/B Testing

A/B testing is a powerful tool for experimentation. By comparing different versions of a product feature or marketing strategy, you can determine which one performs better. Use A/B testing to optimize user experience and make informed decisions based on data. This method provides concrete evidence of what works, helping you make strategic choices that drive success.

Document and Share Learnings

Encourage teams to document the results of their experiments and share their learnings with the rest of the organization. This helps build a knowledge base and ensures that valuable insights are not lost. Regularly reviewing and discussing these learnings can identify patterns and opportunities for further improvement. Sharing knowledge across the organization fosters a culture of collective learning and continuous enhancement.

By integrating these strategies, you can cultivate an environment where experimentation thrives, driving innovation and continuous improvement. This culture of experimentation not only supports the success of your pivot but also ensures your organization remains adaptable and forward-thinking in the face of future challenges.

Embracing Failure as a Learning Opportunity

Failure is an inevitable part of experimentation, but it can also be a valuable learning opportunity. Here’s how to embrace failure and turn it into a positive experience:

Normalize Failure

Normalize failure by acknowledging that it is a natural part of the innovation process. Communicate that failures are expected and can provide valuable insights for future success. By creating an environment where failure is seen as a step towards growth rather than a setback, you encourage a culture of experimentation and risk-taking.

Conduct Post-Mortems

After a failed experiment, conduct a post-mortem analysis to understand what went wrong and why. Identify the root causes of the failure and document the lessons learned. Use this information to make improvements and avoid similar mistakes in the future. Post-mortems provide a structured way to dissect failures and extract valuable insights that can inform future projects.

Foster Resilience

Encourage resilience by supporting team members through setbacks and helping them bounce back from failures. Provide the necessary resources and guidance to help them learn from their experiences and move forward. By fostering a supportive environment, you enable your team to handle failures constructively and maintain their motivation and drive.

By normalizing failure, conducting thorough post-mortems, and fostering resilience, you can transform setbacks into valuable learning opportunities. This approach not only enhances individual and team growth but also strengthens your organization's ability to innovate and adapt in a constantly changing market.

Continuous Learning and Improvement

Continuous learning and improvement are essential for staying competitive in a rapidly changing market. Here are some strategies to promote ongoing learning and development:

Establish Feedback Loops

Create feedback loops to gather input from customers, team members, and other stakeholders. Use this feedback to identify areas for improvement and make data-driven decisions. Regularly reviewing feedback and incorporating it into your product development process ensures that you remain responsive to user needs and can continually enhance your product.

Monitor Industry Trends

Stay updated with industry trends and best practices by following relevant publications, attending conferences, and participating in professional networks. Using this information to inform your strategies helps you stay ahead of the competition and ensures that your team is aware of the latest advancements and opportunities in your field.

Invest in Technology and Tools

Invest in the latest technology and tools that can enhance your product development and experimentation processes. Utilize data analytics, automation, and other advanced technologies to streamline workflows and gain deeper insights. By leveraging cutting-edge tools, you can optimize your processes and make more informed decisions that drive innovation and efficiency.

Encourage Cross-Functional Collaboration

Promote cross-functional collaboration to leverage diverse perspectives and expertise. Encourage teams to work together on projects and share their knowledge and skills. This collaboration fosters innovation and helps identify new opportunities for improvement. When team members from different departments collaborate, they bring unique insights and ideas that can lead to more comprehensive and effective solutions.

By implementing these strategies, you can cultivate a culture of continuous learning and improvement. This approach not only enhances individual and team growth but also ensures that your organization remains agile and competitive in a rapidly evolving market.

Case Studies: Fostering a Culture of Experimentation and Continuous Learning

Google is renowned for its culture of experimentation and continuous learning. The company encourages employees to spend 20% of their time on passion projects, which has led to the development of successful products like Gmail and Google Maps. Google also conducts numerous A/B tests to optimize its products and uses data-driven insights to inform its strategies. This commitment to experimentation allows Google to stay at the forefront of innovation and continually improve its offerings.

Amazon's culture of innovation is driven by continuous experimentation and learning. The company regularly tests new ideas, gathers customer feedback, and iterates on its products and services. Amazon’s commitment to learning from failures and making data-driven decisions has contributed to its success as a global e-commerce leader. By embracing a mindset that values experimentation, Amazon can swiftly adapt to market changes and customer needs.

Netflix fosters a culture of experimentation by encouraging teams to test new ideas and learn from the results. The company uses A/B testing extensively to optimize its user experience and content recommendations. Netflix also invests in employee development and promotes a growth mindset, ensuring that the team remains innovative and adaptable. This approach has helped Netflix maintain its position as a leading streaming service by continually enhancing its platform based on data-driven insights.

Fostering a culture of experimentation and continuous learning is essential for sustaining long-term success after a pivot. By embracing a growth mindset, encouraging experimentation, learning from failures, and promoting ongoing development, you can ensure that your team remains innovative and adaptable. Continuous improvement is a journey, not a destination. The final chapter will summarize the key takeaways from this book and provide a roadmap for navigating change and building successful products in the future.

APPENDIX

This appendix serves as a supplementary resource for readers of "The Art of the Pivot: How to Navigate Change and Build Successful Products." It includes additional tools, templates, case studies, and glossaries that complement the content found within the book. The goal of this appendix is to provide practical resources that can be directly applied to enhance understanding and implementation of the strategies discussed.

A. Pivot Tools and Templates

Strategic Pivot Planning Template: A step-by-step guide to help product managers formulate and execute pivot strategies.

Stakeholder Communication Plan Template: A template to structure and organize communication efforts with stakeholders during a pivot.

Risk Assessment Matrix: A tool to identify, evaluate, and mitigate risks associated with a pivot.

User Feedback Survey Template: A questionnaire to gather valuable insights from users about their needs and experiences.

Product Repositioning Checklist: A checklist outlining key steps and considerations when repositioning a product in the market.

B. Detailed Case Studies

Slack's Transformation: Examines Slack's pivot from a game development company to a leading team communication platform, highlighting key decisions and strategies.

Netflix's Shift to Streaming: Explores Netflix's successful pivot from a DVD rental service to a global streaming giant, detailing the challenges and strategic moves involved.

Airbnb's Market Expansion: Analyzes how Airbnb expanded its market beyond home-sharing to include various types of accommodations, and the impact of this strategic shift.

C. Glossary of Terms

Agile Methodologies: A set of principles for software development under which requirements and solutions evolve through the collaborative effort of self-organizing cross-functional teams.

Customer Acquisition Cost (CAC): The total cost of acquiring a new customer, including marketing and sales expenses.

Customer Lifetime Value (CLTV): The total revenue a customer is expected to generate over their lifetime with your product.

Minimum Viable Product (MVP): A product with just enough features to satisfy early customers and provide feedback for future product development.

Net Promoter Score (NPS): A measure of customer loyalty and likelihood to recommend your product to others.

Pivot: A strategic change in direction for a product or business, typically to adapt to market changes or new opportunities.

D. Recommended Reading and Resources

To further enhance your understanding and skills in pivoting, product management, and related topics, here are some recommended readings and resources:

Books:

- "The Lean Startup: How Today's Entrepreneurs Use Continuous Innovation to Create Radically Successful Businesses" by Eric Ries - Offers strategies for efficient business model testing and development.
- "Measure What Matters: OKRs: The Simple Idea that Drives 10x Growth" by John Doerr - Discusses the importance of setting and measuring objectives and key results.
- "Crossing the Chasm: Marketing and Selling High-Tech Products to Mainstream Customers" by Geoffrey A. Moore - Explores strategies for taking disruptive innovations to mainstream markets.
- "Innovator's Dilemma: When New Technologies Cause Great Firms to Fail" by Clayton M. Christensen - Analyzes why large companies often fail to innovate successfully.

Journals:

- Harvard Business Review: Offers articles on innovation, strategy, and leadership.
- Journal of Product Innovation Management: Provides insights on new product development and management practices.
- MIT Sloan Management Review: Discusses strategies and research on management practices.

Online Resources:

- MIT Sloan Management Review (https://sloanreview.mit.edu/): Provides modern strategies and research on management practices.
- McKinsey Insights (https://www.mckinsey.com/featured-insights): Offers research and articles on various business management topics.
- Product School Blog (https://www.productschool.com/blog/): Provides articles and resources on product management and development.

"The measure of intelligence is the ability to change."
— Albert Einstein

"It is not the strongest of the species that survive, nor the most intelligent, but the one most responsive to change."
— Charles Darwin

"Success is not the result of spontaneous combustion. You must set yourself on fire."
— Arnold H. Glasow

"In a time of drastic change, it is the learners who inherit the future. The learned usually find themselves equipped to live in a world that no longer exists."
— Eric Hoffer

"Change is the law of life. And those who look only to the past or present are certain to miss the future."
— John F. Kennedy

"The greatest danger in times of turbulence is not the turbulence; it is to act with yesterday's logic."
— Peter Drucker

"Innovation distinguishes between a leader and a follower."
— Steve Jobs

www.ingramcontent.com/pod-product-compliance
Lightning Source LLC
LaVergne TN
LVHW090122160826
845673LV00015B/819

* 9 7 8 2 3 8 7 8 3 3 1 4 3 *